FITNESS

Written By:
Herbert I. Kavet

Illustrated By:
Martin Riskin

Ivory Tower Publishing Co., Inc.
125 Walnut Street
P.O. Box 9132
Watertown, MA 02272-9132
Telephone #: (617) 923-1111   Fax #: (617) 923-8839

"I bet he'll ask for help next time
before using the new machines."

"Sylvia is <u>so</u> serious about her aerobics."

Dressing For Fitness

There are two kinds of outfits you can wear for your workout.

1. Show it if you've got it — In this case you wear lycra, spandex and nylon so everyone can see exactly what you've got.

2. Hide it if you don't — Baggy sweat suits, fleece, cotton and canvas are the bywords here.

"I don't know who that is, but every now and then it moves."

Early Kenyans learn about fitness that later prepares them to run marathons.

"How come you never jog?"

No Pain, No Gain vs.
It Can't Be Bad If It Feels Good

Those of the "no pain, no gain" school of thought lift heavy weights, swim, row, run and ride prodigious distances. They generally smell up health clubs and have hard, little asses. The "can't be bad if it feels good" people hang out in the hot tubs, saunas and bars. They smell like roses, are generally cuddly, and tend to have soft, round tushes.

"Laps in the hot tub don't count."

"Everything that was fattening is now a health food."

Health Clubs

The cutest guy or gal is always positioned at the front desk to give you an example of what you, too, can become. The other instructors may be ugly as dogs or even overweight themselves, but they are always well-hidden in the back rooms. You don't see them until after you've joined.

The gods and goddesses at the front desk collect your money and guard entry from all whose payments are overdue. It's very embarrassing when they throw you out in front of members you were trying to impress. Remember, during your mortification, that the attendant at the front desk is even more underpaid than you. Bribes are always effective and can even get you an extra towel.

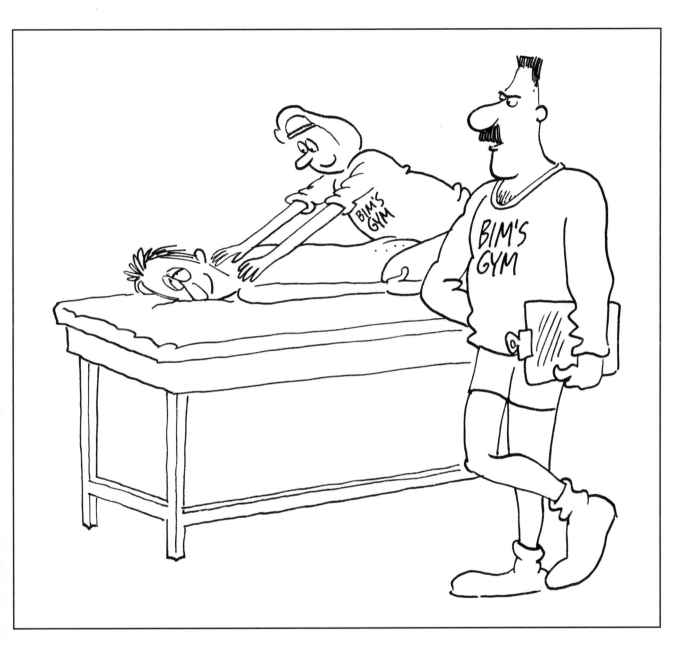

"I don't notice you putting the massage and steam
bath in your training log."

"Wayne is an afternoon member and Sam can only do aerobics, but Dennis can go on weekends, and Harry's allowed to use the pool, but only before 6:00."

God created the one-size pantyhose so women would remember their New Year's resolution to get more exercise and lose weight.

Basic Workout Principles

1. Always warm-up and stretch before exercising, but avoid bending your body into positions you may not be able to get out of.

2. A good sauna or steam bath is worth 30 minutes of sweating with weights.

3. You can double the value of a hot tub by turning the bubbles on.

4. A nap of any duration benefits the body as much as 15 minutes on the Stairmaster.

5. Good sex has a cardiovascular effect equal to a 3 mile run. (Bad sex is equal to a 2 mile run).

6. Listening to rock music doubles the value of any exercise.

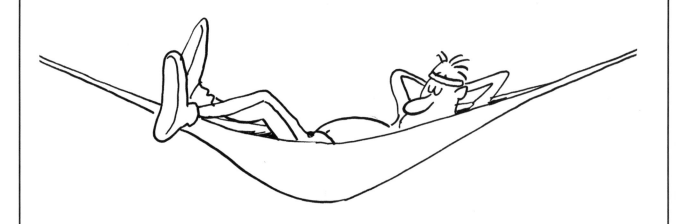

Basic Diet Principles

1. Calories don't count if you snack while exercising.
2. It's important to carbo load before and after a workout.
3. Drink lots to replace body fluids.
4. Control top pantyhose is worth 2,364 sit-ups.

Nautilus And Other Exercise Machines

Anything with this much chrome and imitation leather that promises to isolate muscle groups and build them up to prodigious proportions can't be all bad. The only problem with this equipment comes from working out in a small puddle of the last user's sweat. Many clubs suggest you carry a towel to mop up your sweat, but only new members bother.

Fears of getting caught in these machines and grinding various parts of yourself into hamburger have been greatly exaggerated. Hang gliding, Middle East Terrorists and shark diving are all probably far more dangerous.

"No, no, Mr. Michelson! After you put the weights on the bar, you lift it."

"This is our lowest impact aerobics class."

"Igor has had wonderful success improving other members with limited flexibility."

Why Men Take Aerobics Classes

Come on, you all know. What, with all that jiggling and tight lycra, it's no wonder these poor fellows have trouble with their flexibility. 94% of men in aerobics classes come to watch the women, only they call them "girls" in the locker room, and the other 6% are in love with the instructor.

"And what do you folks do to maintain your cardiovascular fitness?"

When Sumo wrestlers go into the jacuzzi.

"You mean I've already satisfied 100% of my
daily requirement?"

How To Fart In An Aerobics Class

A fart is embarrassing in any public circumstance and much more so in the closed confines of an aerobics class. All the jumping around tends to jiggle these little fellows out of your system and is the primary reason why the music is played so loudly at most clubs.

There are 3 ways to handle the problem.

1. Flap your arms vigorously to dissipate the odor.

2. Blame it on some other guy or gal.

3. Rapidly vacate the area you have just blasted.

"I sort of look on it as a poor woman's Stairmaster."

"Let's see? That's been 2 recovery days, 1 rest day and 2 carbo loading days this week."

Body Fat Analysis

The best way to do this analysis is to dunk your body in a tub of water and measure how much spills over the top. When you used to do that at home your mother would yell at you, but health care professionals get away with it. This total immersion involves undressing, which is something fat people hate to do, and has been found to be wildly inaccurate for people with fat heads, for example, so the caliper pinch method or some sort of electronic system is mostly used. These studies are very valuable to your fitness program because they tell you just how much of your body is fat, how much M&M's, and how much Ben & Jerry's ice cream.

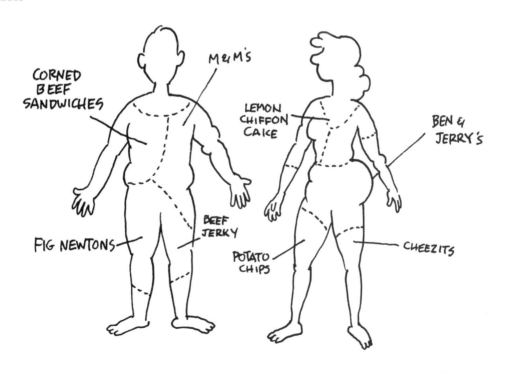

Tennis At A Fitness Club

Remember tennis? About 10 years ago it was the "in" sport (just before racquet ball, aerobics and roller blading). Well, most fitness centers were tennis clubs in those days and most still have the courts. If you use these courts, watch out for two main hazards.

---

1. Avoid, at all costs, all courts adjoining a lesson. That court will have 10,000 semi-dead balls rolling around as the Pro tosses them at the pupil. You'll spend most of your hour watching your new balls roll towards the adjoining court where they will disappear.

Tennis At A Fitness Club

2. Even worse than playing next to a lesson is being assigned to <u>COURT #1</u>. The diabolical kid at the desk will put you here when your game is off and your outfit the rattiest. Unless you are an experienced, ranked competitor, the thought of all those people watching will destroy your game. Anyone you've ever tried to impress in the locker room or lounge will be standing behind the glass window snickering at you.

"Howard's training log says he ran 27 miles last week, but he really ran 24."

Maria has this recurring nightmare about being
in the wrong locker room.

Locker Logic

Every club's locker has the following 5 characteristics:

1. It's a little smaller than the total of what you want to put into it.

2. The door only closes if you whack it.

3. It's numbered in some unfathomable system.

4. A ripe odor invariably emanates, possibly from...

5. A torn pair of dirty underwear always crumpled in the back corner, or an indescribably greasy comb on the floor.

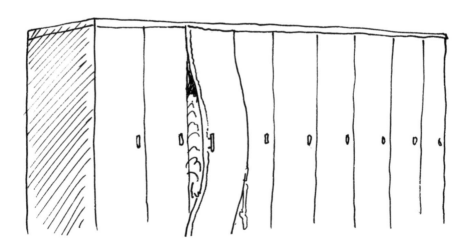

Locker Logic

No matter how many lockers are available and how large the facility, there will be a small crowd of people either dripping sweat, or water, or dusting you with talcum powder as you all gather by adjoining lockers.

"Well, those are my aerobic shoes, and those my running, and those my shower clogs, and those my tennis sneakers, and those my basketball....."

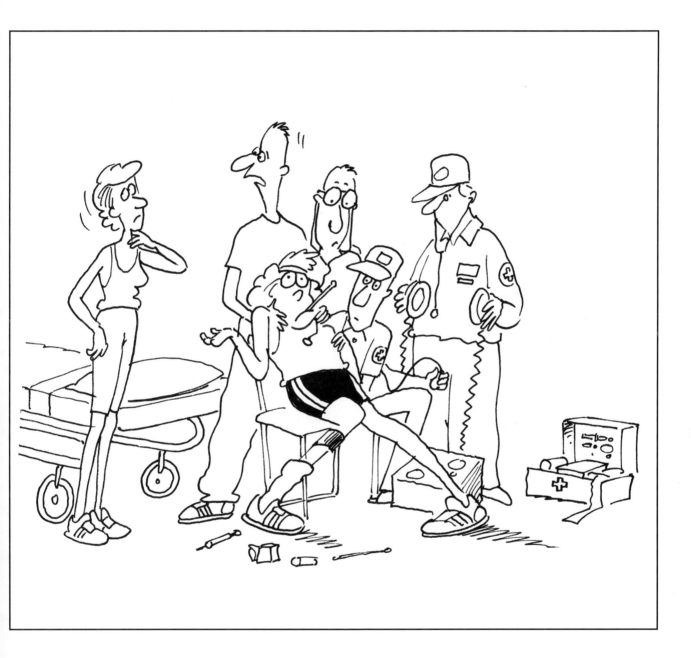

"Marilyn couldn't find her pulse so we decided not to take any chances."

Naked Bodies

You'll see more raw nudity in a locker room or shower than anywhere else. These places are a cornucopia of flesh, weird underwear and unusual personal habits. A careful observer will notice that men are made mostly of hair and maybe 10% aftershave lotion. Women consist more of baby powder and eye make-up and are held together by pantyhose.

"Mom, Grandpa's bothering the women
joggers again."

"Whaddaya mean I have to push them myself!"

"Doesn't anyone just splash around anymore?"

Health Club Bulletin Boards

If anyone followed all the tips and advice diets and workouts on these boards, they wouldn't have time to sleep, much less go to work. "Everyone should stretch in the morning, 20 stretches, hold each for 20 seconds, 5 times on each side of your body." Then you go into grinding your own sesame seeds for breakfast once you've finished the repeat sprints that are recommended after a 6 mile warm-up run. You haven't even got to the section on weights for strength training, cross training with swimming and roller blades, fifteen great calve exercises on the Stairmaster, and stomach workouts that should be done twice a day.

Leona believes the weight loss claims of the new
health club and immediately buys new lycra outfits.

George's greatest fear was that one day the entire stretching class would turn around and realize just how little he had progressed.

"We're only behind 2 points. Don't anyone
lose their head."

Fitness While Traveling

Northwest Airlines has this seat aerobics routine they play on planes at the end of long flights. Doing them is a great way to convince the seat mate you were trying to impress, that you are indeed a complete idiot.

Most good hotels also have jogging route maps in the room. If you follow these maps very carefully they will keep you out of the really bad neighborhoods where you would be murdered on sight, leaving you instead with the problem of dealing with the stares of the normally dressed people in the elevator.

Gerry realizes the other guests might not
understand his "good luck" socks.

"All right, all right. I'm sure everyone has seen
somebody throw-up on the treadmill before."

"Are you sure no one is chasing them?"

Personal Trainers

This is where your "instructor" is called a "personal trainer" and comes to your home or gym and exhorts you to greater efforts, all the time trying to keep you from falling too much in love with them because they are usually very attractive members of the opposite sex. Personal trainers make you keep training logs and records of your weight and generally introduce a whole new set of situations you'll want to lie and cheat to yourself about.

"Somebody should report this to the Society For
The Prevention of Cruelty to Spandex."

To her eternal embarrassment, Elizabeth's snack slipped out as soon as they started the leg raises.

Why Nobody Ever Loses Weight On A Home Exercise Device

The home exercise equipment market is now worth about $40 billion a year and none of this stuff has ever been used past the first week. These shiny weight machines, stationary bikes, rowing, skiing and climbing devices clutter up family rooms, garages and cellars across America and no one understands why people keep spending money for them when your neighbor will gladly pay you just to take the thing out of the way of their TV set.

Most of Cindy's fitness program revolved around
loading exercise tapes into her VCR.

"I'm beginning to wonder if this is such a great way to meet men?"

Knees And Fitness

Many exercise programs are sponsored by Sports Medicine Professionals to ensure a steady supply of knee injuries for their businesses. Any sport involving standing, running or bending is made to order for these doctors. When you get your knee injury, which happens in 73% of all cases, they pretend to cure it with orthoscopic surgery. In this procedure, if you can believe it, they cut a little hole in your knee and make believe they're roto-rooting out the bad stuff in the middle. Forget about leading a normally active life after visiting any of these people.

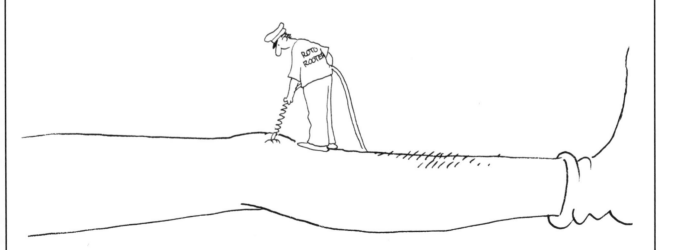

"Jackie, explain to me again how those endorphins work!"

Endorphins

Endorphins are hormones that are secreted, when you exercise, from your pituitary gland directly into your brain. I'm not making this up. These endorphins give you a great euphoric feeling similar to morphine and other restricted substances. This is where a "runner's high" comes from. When the government finds out about these endorphins, you can bet they'll make them illegal and lock you up if you're found having any in your brain.

Sidney was sure his exercise program would help him lose weight and would change his whole social life.

Learning To Eat Potato Chips And Watch TV Again

Deprogramming groups are available to teach exercise nuts how to relax and enjoy themselves again. The groups provide fat-filled snack foods and help people to become socially acceptable, happy, couch potatoes. Most states have federal funds to help with these programs and when you grow tired of this fitness nonsense you should contact them.

These other books are available at many fine stores.

#2350 Sailing. Using the head at night • Sex & Sailing • Monsters in the Ice Chest • How to look nautical in bars and much more nautical nonsense.

#2351 Computers. Where computers really are made • How to understand computer manuals without reading them • Sell your old $2,000,000 computer for $60 • Why computers are always lonely and much more solid state computer humor.

#2352 Cats. Living with cat hair • The advantages of kitty litter • Cats that fart • How to tell if you've got a fat cat.

#2353 Tennis. Where do lost balls go? • Winning the psychological game • Catching your breath • Perfecting wood shots.

#2354 Bowling. A book of bowling cartoons that covers: Score sheet cheaters • Boozers • Women who show off • Facing your team after a bad box and much more.

#2355 Parenting. Understanding the Tooth Fairy • 1000 ways to toilet train • Informers and tattle tales • Differences between little girls and little boys • And enough other information and laughs to make every parent wet their beds.

#2356 Fitness. T-shirts that will stop them from laughing at you • Earn big money with muscles • Sex and Fitness • Lose weight with laughter from this book.

#2357 Golf. Playing the psychological game • Going to the toilet in the rough • How to tell a real golfer • Some of the best golf cartoons ever printed.

#2358 Fishing. Handling 9" mosquitoes • Raising worms in your microwave oven • Neighborhood targets for fly casting practice • How to get on a first name basis with the Coast Guard plus even more.

#2359 Bathrooms. Why people love their bathroom • Great games to help pass the time on toilets • A frank discussion of bathroom odors • Plus lots of other stuff everyone out of diapers should know.

#2360 Biking. Why the wind is always against you • Why bike clothes are so tight • And lots of other stuff about what goes thunk, thunk, thunk when you pedal.

#2361 Running. How to "go" in the woods • Why running shoes cost more than sneakers • Keeping your lungs from bursting by letting the other guy talk.

Ivory Tower Publishing Co., Inc.   125 Walnut St., PO Box 9132, Watertown, MA 02272-9132
Telephone #: (617) 923-1111   Fax #: (617) 923-8839